Note to Parents/Guardians, Teachers, Counselors, & Other Caring Professionals

The purpose of this workbook is to help children better understand their feelings, and practice strategies for dealing with those feelings in a socially appropriate manner. This book is written for elementary school age children, but may be of use for those younger or older.

In so many books and studies I have read about children and adults with mental health problems, there is a strong tie between an inability to manage emotions and problems with day to day functioning. My desire with this workbook is to help all children build more resilience to life's problems by better understanding their own emotions and responding to those emotions in healthy and adaptive ways. This book should be particularly helpful for those children with a mental health diagnosis.

My hope is that this book facilitates discussions with your child to help in that process. In using this book, help the child understand that feelings are an emotional response to stimulus, and it's very hard, if not impossible, to change those initial feelings. What a child can learn to do, however, is manage the resulting behavior. In other words, while it is acceptable to be angry, it is not acceptable to act destructively because of that anger. It may not be easy, but it is possible.

I hope you and your child find this workbook empowering, helpful, and even a little fun. I welcome your comments. For additional books and resources, please visit www.bpchildren.com.

Bryna Hebert

© Copyright 2008, Bryna Hebert
Images on pages 30, 31, 39, 40, 54, 55, 71, 77, 78, 82: BigStockPhoto.com © Dawn Hudson
Image on page 72: BigStockPhoto.com © Andrzej Windak
All rights reserved.
ISBN 978-0-9817396-1-8
Published by BPChildren, Murdock, Fl
www.bpchildren.com

Table of Contents

About Me

This book belongs to:_____

It was given to me by:_____ on _____, 20_____

I am _____ years old, and I am in the _____ grade.

I have _____ sisters and _____ brothers, and I live with my _____

_____

My favorite color is _____

My best friends are _____

_____

My favorite thing in school is _____

I am very good at _____

_____

Adults like me because _____

_____

Kids like me because _____

_____

My favorite place to go is_____

_____

My favorite thing to do is _____

_____

My best memory is _____

_____

_____

A lot of people love me. They are:_____

_____

_____

These things are important to me:_____

_____

_____

Other Things About Me: _____

_____

_____

Feelings

This section of the workbook is designed to help you understand your feelings better by describing what your face might look like, how your body might feel, and the thoughts you might have when you feel those feelings. Being able to understand what you are feeling can help you make healthy choices about what to do about those feelings.

> ➤ What does a happy face look like?

A happy face has a smile, round eyes that look straight ahead or up, and straight eyebrows.

> ➤ What does a happy body feel like?

A happy body feels bouncy or like skipping, dancing, or singing. Sometimes a happy body needs to hug someone else or do a high five.

> ➤ What do happy thoughts sound like?

"Wow, this is great!"

"Yeah! We're going to Grandma's house tomorrow."

"Yahoo, I'm going to my friend's house after school!"

> ➤ What are some of the things that make me happy?

_____

_____

_____

> ➤ What are some other words for happy?

_____

_____

Bored

➤ What does a bored face look like?

The eyes are dull and droopy, eyebrows are plain, and the mouth almost frowns. Sometimes the face starts looking impatient or frustrated too.

➤ What does a bored body feel like?

Like it wants to do something fun or even like it wants to jump out of its skin.

➤ What do bored thoughts sound like?

"I want to play with someone."

"I'm bored."

"If it rains one more day, I'm going to lose it!"

➤ What makes me bored?

_____

_____

➤ What are some other words for bored?

_____

_____

➤ What can I do when I'm bored?

_____

_____

_____

➢ What does a sad face look like?

A sad face has eyes that look downward, straight eyebrows, and a mouth with corners that go down instead of up. Sometimes a sad face has tears.

➢ What does a sad body feel like?

A sad body is tired and slumps—shoulders sag, your back slouches, and you walk kind of slow and without energy.

➢ What do sad thoughts sound like?

"Nobody loves me."

"I miss my dog."

➢ What makes me sad?

_____

_____

➢ What are some other words for sad?

_____

_____

➢ What makes me feel better when I'm sad?

_____

_____

_____

calm

➤ **What does a calm face look like?**

A calm face has a straight mouth, straight eyebrows, and eyes that are open and look ahead. Muscles are relaxed and the face might even look a little happy.

➤ **What does a calm body feel like?**

A calm body is relaxed and feels like a bowl of pudding. Your hands are relaxed, your shoulders are low, and you probably aren't moving very much.

➤ **What do calm thoughts sound like?**

"I feel calm and relaxed."

"_____"   (in other words, your mind is completely blank)

"Nothing can bother me now."

➤ **What are some of the sights, sounds, smells, activities, or things that make me feel calm?**

_____

_____

➤ **What are some other words for calm?**

_____

FRUSTRATED!

➢ What does a frustrated face look like?

The eyes get squinty, eyebrows are squished together, and the mouth gets small. Sometimes the face looks angry too.

➢ What does a frustrated body feel like?

Like it wants to stomp its feet, hit something, or like it's going to explode. The stomach might be tight, and hands want to do something. There's a lot of energy, but it's angry, not fun.

➢ What do frustrated thoughts sound like?

"I hate doing this!"

"I want it now!"

"AAAArgh!"

➢ What makes me frustrated?

_____

_____

➢ What are some other words for frustrated?

_____

_____

➢ What helps me when I'm feeling frustrated?

_____

_____

DISAPPOINTED

➤ **What does a disappointed face look like?**

It looks a little sad and sometimes a little angry, too.

➤ **What does a disappointed body feel like?**

Like it wants to cry or stomp its feet.

➤ **What do disappointed thoughts sound like?**

"I can't believe it's raining – I wanted to go to the beach."

"I'm so bummed that he can't come over to play. Now I'm going to be bored."

"I thought the fair was going to be fun, but it was just loud and dirty."

➤ **What makes me feel disappointed?**

_____

_____

➤ **What are some other words for disappointed?**

_____

_____

➤ **What can I do when I'm disappointed?**

_____

_____

CONFIDENT

➤ What does a confident face look like?

The eyes are bright and open, the eyebrows are straight, and the mouth sometimes smiles.

➤ What does a confident body feel like?

Like it's strong, tall, and courageous. Sometimes the hands are on the hips or arms raised up in the air.

➤ What do confident thoughts sound like?

"I can do it!"

"I am smart!"

"I am brave!"

➤ What makes me feel confident?

_____

_____

_____

_____

➤ What are some other words for confident?

_____

_____

_____

Lonely...

➢ What does a lonely face look like?

It looks sad. The eyes look down, the ends of the mouth are down, and sometimes the eyebrows go up in the middle. Sometimes, the eyes are crying too.

➢ What does a lonely body feel like?

Like it needs a hug or a laugh. It slumps a little or maybe even curls up in a ball.

➢ What do lonely thoughts sound like?

"I wish someone could play."

"No one understands me."

"I wish I had more friends."

➢ What makes me feel lonely?

_____

_____

_____

➢ What are some other words for lonely?

_____

_____

➢ What helps me when I'm feeling lonely?

_____

_____

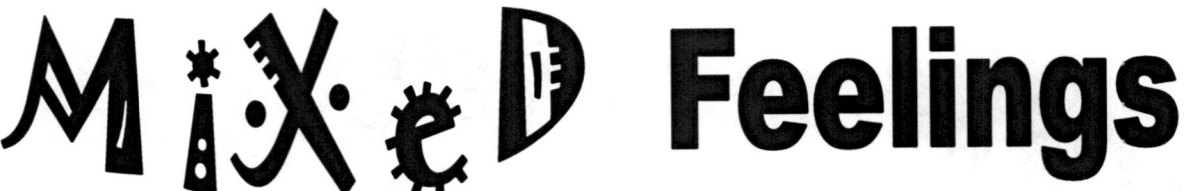

Mixed Feelings

➤ **What are mixed feelings?**

When you have more than one feeling at a time. Like when you are excited to see your friends on the first day of school, but you're worried your new teacher won't like you.

➤ **What does a mixed feeling face look like?**

The expression on your face may change up and back, like from happy to worried and back again, or it might just look confused, because it isn't sure how it feels.

➤ **What does a mixed feeling body feel like?**

Like it wants to cartwheel one minute and slump into a chair the next.

➤ **What do mixed thoughts sound like?**

"I was so excited for school to start yesterday, but now I don't want to go."

"I like going to see Grandma & Grandpa, but I hate the long drive."

"I like being up in an airplane, but coming down scares me."

➤ **What gives me mixed feelings?**

_____

_____

➤ **What are some other words for mixed feelings?**

_____

_____

➤ **What helps me when I don't know how I feel?**

_____

_____

Scared

➢ **What does a scared face look like?**

The eyes are wide open, eyebrows pointing up, and edges of the mouth pointing down. The jaw might be shaking.

➢ **What does a scared body feel like?**

Tight, arms held close to the body, sometimes up by the mouth and ready to cover your eyes.

➢ **What do scared thoughts sound like?**

"It's too dark in here."

"There's no way I can get up in front of the whole class."

"What if the lightning hits the house?"

➢ **What makes me feel scared?**

_____

_____

➢ **What are some other words for scared?**

_____

_____

➢ **What makes me feel better when I'm scared?**

_____

_____

_____

BRAVE

➤ **What does a brave face look like?**

The eyes are bright and focused, the eyebrows are mostly straight, but a little squished together, and the mouth is straight and determined.

➤ **What does a brave body feel like?**

It feels strong, ready, and confident.

➤ **What do brave thoughts sound like?**

"I can do this!"

"I'm not afraid to try this."

"I'm going to go into the basement all by myself."

➤ **What makes me feel brave?**

_____

_____

_____

_____

➤ **What are some other words for brave?**

_____

_____

_____

ANGRY

➤ **What does an angry face look like?**

Eyebrows are scrunched down, mouth is straight or corners are down, eyes are small, and sometimes the skin starts turning red.

➤ **What does an angry body feel like?**

Tense – hands might be in fists or arms crossed across the body. Sometimes the body wants to hit something or someone and is full of angry energy. Sometimes the body gets hot, starts sweating, and thoughts start racing.

➤ **What do angry thoughts sound like?**

"I hate him!"

"I'm so mad!"

"My teacher is so mean!"

➤ **What makes me angry?**

_____

_____

➤ **What are some other words for angry?**

_____

_____

➤ **What makes me feel better when I'm angry?**

_____

_____

_____

Embarrassed

➤ What does an embarrassed face look like?

The eyes are wide open, the eyebrows go up at the middle, the mouth gets small or frowns, and sometimes the cheeks or whole face turns red. Sometimes the face then cries or looks angry.

➤ What does an embarrassed body feel like?

Like it wants to hide or hurt the person that made it feel embarrassed.

➤ What do embarrassed thoughts sound like?

"Why did I say that? I'm so stupid!"

"I can't believe my underwear was showing. I just want to hide."

"Why did he trick me into being scared like a baby? I can't show my face there again."

➤ What makes me feel embarrassed?

_____

_____

➤ What are some other words for embarrassed?

_____

_____

➤ What helps me when I'm embarrassed?

_____

_____

_____

 Surprised

➢ **What does a surprised face look like?**

Eyes are wide open, the mouth is open like a circle, and the eyebrows are pointing up. Depending on whether it's a good surprise, a scary surprise, or an annoying surprise, the face could also look happy, scared, or angry.

➢ **What does a surprised body feel like?**

A little tense if it's a scary surprise and bouncy if it's a happy surprise.

➢ **What do surprised thoughts sound like?**

"Whoa!"

"Ahhhhhhhh!"

"What?!"

➢ **What makes me feel surprised?**

_____

_____

➢ **What are some other words for surprised?**

_____

➢ **What can I do when I'm surprised?**

_____

_____

_____

WORRIED

➤ **What does a worried face look like?**

Uncertain, cautious, quiet, and not knowing how to react or what to do. The eyes are open, but the eyebrows may be down. The mouth might be trembling.

➤ **What does a worried body feel like?**

A little tense, a little jumpy, and a little shaky. Knees might shake and the tummy might be upset or feel like it's in knots.

➤ **What do worried thoughts sound like?**

"What if I don't get a 100 on my spelling test today?"

"What if Billy will never play with me again?"

"What if I don't get a hit and the team doesn't win the game?"

➤ **What makes me feel worried?**

_____

_____

➤ **What are some other words for worried?**

_____

_____

➤ **What makes me feel better when I'm worried?**

_____

_____

_____

More Feelings

Sometimes kids with challenges have more and stronger feelings than other kids. The next couple of pages describe these feelings.

Impulsive

➢ **What does an impulsive face look like?**

It can have any of the emotions. Being impulsive means that you do something before you think it through, so you could be happy, sad, angry, or frustrated.

➢ **What does an impulsive body feel like?**

A little like it's out of control and doing things on its own, without waiting for directions from you. For example, hands that can't stop touching things.

➢ **What do impulsive thoughts sound like?**

"That looks like fun."

"I wonder what it's like to fly..."

"I want that now!"

➢ **When am I impulsive?**

_____

_____

➢ **What are some other words for impulsive?**

_____

_____

➢ **What can I do to be less impulsive?**

_____

_____

_____

Hyper

➤ **What does a hyper face look like?**

It might be super excited or lost in a daydream.

➤ **What does a hyper body feel like?**

Like it can't stop moving. Toes are tapping, fingers are snapping, sometimes you fall right off a chair.

➤ **What do hyper thoughts sound like?**

"I could run to the moon and back."

"I've got to move NOW"

"First, I'm going to ride my bike, then I'm going to swim, and then I'm going to play basketball."

➤ **When am I hyper?**

_____

_____

➤ **What are some other words for hyper?**

_____

_____

➤ **What can I do to be less hyper?**

_____

EuPhOrIc (you-for-ick)

➢ What does a euphoric face look like?

It looks very very happy. Eyes are sparkling and there is such an enormous smile that the eyes might almost be closed.

➢ What does a euphoric body feel like?

It feels like singing and skipping and jumping and flying. Being euphoric feels really good; but for kids with bipolar disorder, it can be a sign that mania is coming.

➢ What do euphoric thoughts sound like?

"This is the best day of my life!"

"I've never felt so good before!"

"I'm so happy I could cry!" (sometimes people say this when their feelings are overwhelming)

➢ When am I euphoric?

_____

_____

➢ What are some other words for euphoric?

_____

_____

➢ What should I do if I'm euphoric?

_____

_____

mAnIc

➤ Sometimes, "happy" goes too far and then I'm manic.

While it may feel fun for me, it can get dangerous or I might embarrass myself or my family.

➤ These are the things I do when I'm manic:_____

_____

_____

_____

OBSESSED STUCK

➤ What does an obsessed/stuck face look like?

It usually looks pretty intense, but might look frustrated, angry, or even happy. The eyes are very focused.

➤ What does an obsessed/stuck body feel like?

It usually feels very tense.

➤ What do obsessed/stuck thoughts sound like?

"I HAVE to go swimming NOW."

"But I *really* want it, please!"

"If I don't see that movie today, I don't know what I will do!"

➤ When do I get stuck?

_____

_____

➤ What are some other words for obsessed/stuck?

_____

_____

➤ What can I do to get unstuck?

_____

_____

DARING

➤ **What does a daring face look like?**

It looks proud and bold, eyes are a little small, eyebrows are pinched together a little bit, and there's a little smile.

➤ **What does a daring body feel like?**

Like it is strong and it can do anything, even fly.

➤ **What do daring thoughts sound like?**

"I'm sure I can ride my skateboard down those stairs."

"I bet I can beat that car to the stop sign."

"If I jump off the roof, I can fly."

➤ **When am I daring?**

_____

_____

_____

➤ **What are some other words for daring?**

_____

_____

➤ **Am I ever dangerous when I feel daring?**

_____

_____

depressed

➢ Sometimes, the sadness gets extreme, and then I'm depressed.

Sometimes people who are depressed may think about or try to hurt themselves or someone else. They may feel that there are no solutions to their problems and feel alone and stuck. That is NEVER the solution to anything—there is a better day around the corner. I need to tell my parents or doctor or another adult I trust if I'm depressed so they can help me.

➢ These are the things I do when I'm depressed:_____

_____

_____

_____

➢ These are the people I can ask for help from when I'm depressed:_____

_____

_____

Note: see the pages titled "Dealing with Feelings" on page 59 for ideas for feeling better.

COMPLETION CERTIFICATE

_____

has completed the feelings section of the workbook

_____
Signature

_____
Date

31

Feelings Detective

Have you ever pretended to be a detective? Detectives look hard to find clues, solve the case, and sometimes catch the bad guys! Here's your chance to be a Feelings Detective. You'll need to look hard to find the clues about how people feel. The clues may be on a person's face, in the way their voice sounds, in their actions, or hiding in a situation. You'll get to solve the case by answering some questions. You might even catch a few feelings out of place! Those feelings are tricky things.

How I Feel...

Circle the word to describe the feelings you have when these things happen. You can circle more than one, or fill in your own word.

1. When my teacher looks happy to see me.

   Happy   Sad   Confused   _____

2. When I get the answer right in class.

   Sad   Proud   Silly   _____

3. When the neighbor kids ask me to play with them.

   Excited   Happy   Nervous   _____

4. When I have a nightmare.

   Calm   Scared   Sad   _____

5. When there is nothing to do.

   Surprised   Bored   Calm   _____

6. When I say the wrong thing in class.

   Stupid   Calm   Nervous   _____

7. When my mom says we can't go shopping for candy.

   Frustrated   Disappointed   Happy   _____

8. When my dad says he's too busy to play with me.

   Lonely   Disappointed   Hurt   _____

9. When my sister calls me "stupid".

   Hurt   Sad   Angry   _____

10. When I think about trying something new.

    Brave   Worried   Nervous   _____

Draw the Face

On this page, fill in the correct facial expression for the feeling below the circle. Most emotions show on our face with our eyes, eyebrows, and mouth, but sometimes also with our forehead or tears.

Example faces:

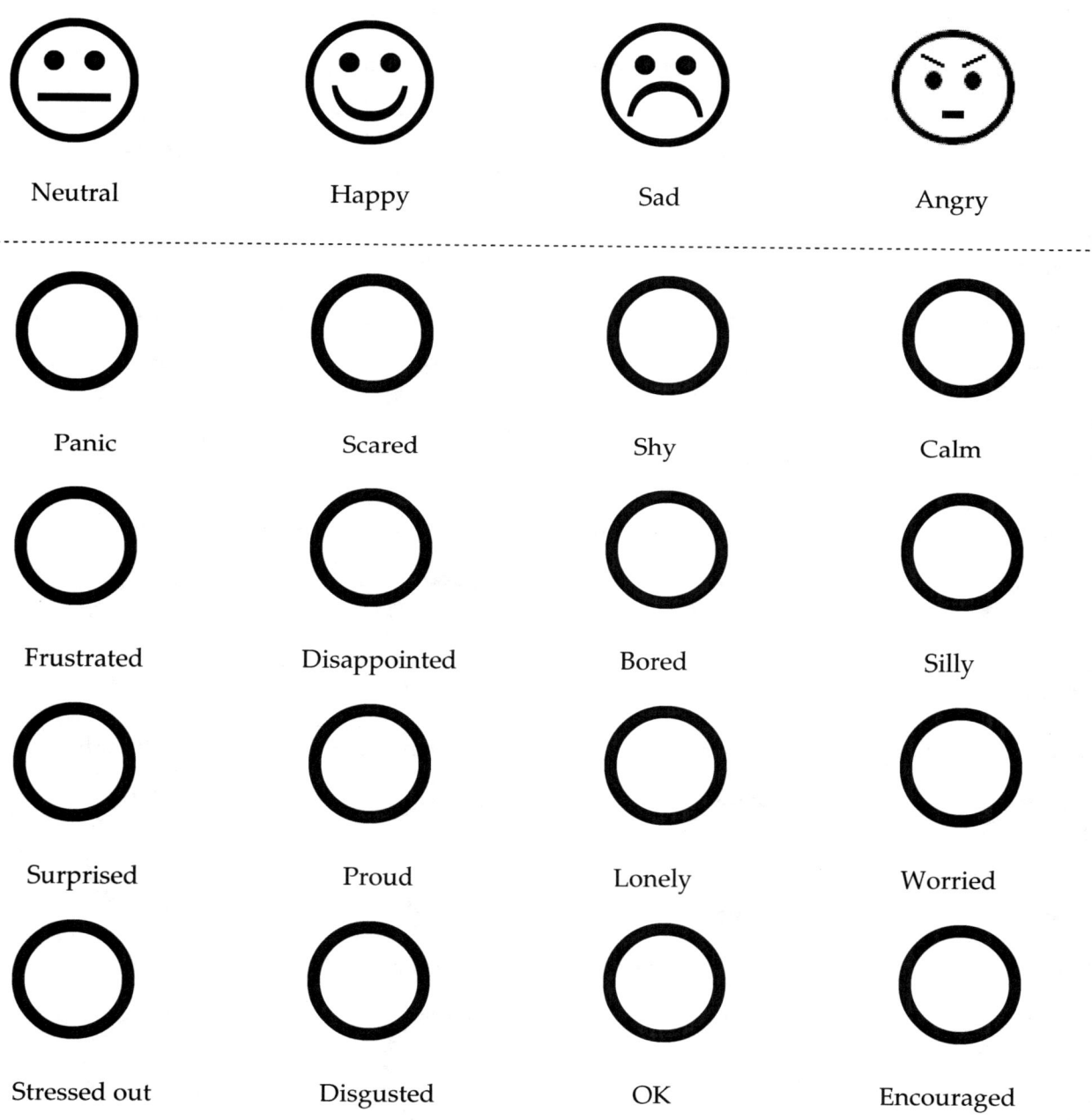

Neutral   Happy   Sad   Angry

Panic   Scared   Shy   Calm

Frustrated   Disappointed   Bored   Silly

Surprised   Proud   Lonely   Worried

Stressed out   Disgusted   OK   Encouraged

How My Face Looks When...

On this page, fill in the way your face looks when you do the following things happen:

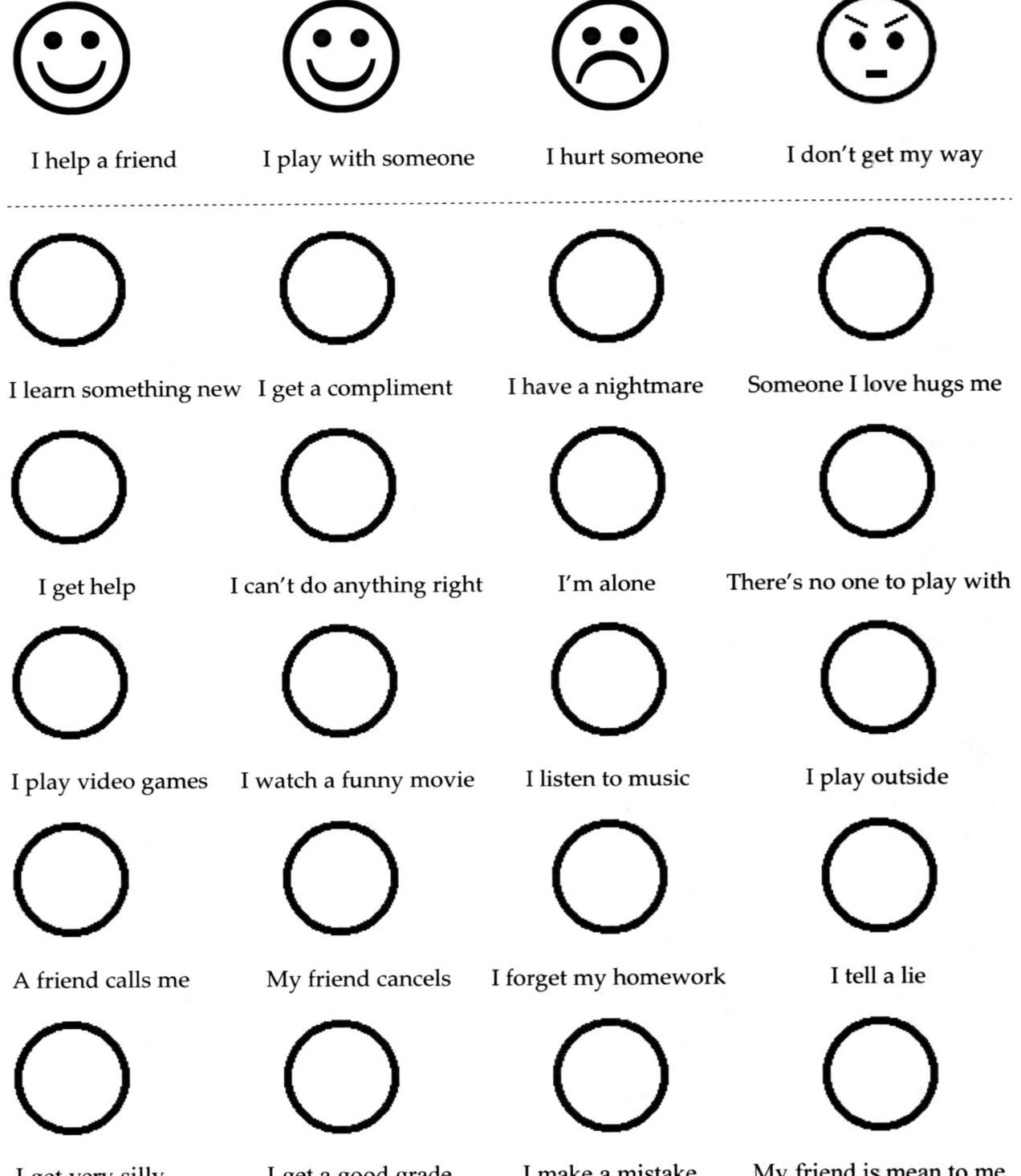

I help a friend   I play with someone   I hurt someone   I don't get my way

I learn something new   I get a compliment   I have a nightmare   Someone I love hugs me

I get help   I can't do anything right   I'm alone   There's no one to play with

I play video games   I watch a funny movie   I listen to music   I play outside

A friend calls me   My friend cancels   I forget my homework   I tell a lie

I get very silly   I get a good grade   I make a mistake   My friend is mean to me

Feelings Story #1

On the next three pages are some stories. In the right hand column is a space to write how you think each person feels during the story and maybe even why. See if you can detect their feelings.

What happened...	How the person felt...
One winter day, a lot of the kids in the neighborhood were playing in the snow. It had snowed a lot the night before and school was closed. Robert looked out the window and got his snow things on. He called to his sisters, "Get out of bed, there's a war going on out there!"	
Robert headed out the door. Nick said, "Be on my team, it's boys against girls!" It was mostly the younger kids in the neighborhood and there were two snow forts with kids throwing snowballs at each other. No one was throwing the snowballs too hard and it was fun.	
Robert's sisters came out and joined the girls team. It was getting very competitive now and Robert got hit in the face once or twice. He was trying to stay cool, but it hurts getting hit in the face.	
Then, some of the older boys from the other end of the street came down to join in. Sometimes they were too rough for the younger kids.	
At first, it was fine, but then they started packing the snowballs really hard. When Robert got hit accidentally by a hard one, he started crying. The older boys started laughing and making fun of him.	
Then, it got really out of hand. The older boys started throwing snowball after snowball at Robert and they thought it was funny. Roberts sister's said "That's more than enough!" While Nick put his sled in front of Robert to stop the snowballs from hitting him, Robert's sisters went and got their mom. The older boys scattered as soon as she opened the door.	
The other kids all came around Robert and told him they felt bad about what happened and suggested that they make a snowman instead. They all worked together and made the biggest snowman ever.	

37

Feelings Story #2

What happened...	How the person felt...
Hannah, Jessica, and Amanda were best friends. They lived on the same street, went to the same school, and like a lot of the same things. They walked to school together every morning and walked home every afternoon.	
One day, Madison, another girl at school, told Amanda that Hannah and Jessica had been saying mean things about her and that they thought she was stupid. Amanda couldn't believe it—how could they do that to her?	
So, the next day at school, Amanda told one of Jessica's secrets to Madison. Madison spread it to three other girls and one of them told Jessica that she knew. Jessica couldn't believe it—how could Amanda do that to her?	
Hannah tried to talk to Amanda to find out what was going on, but Amanda wouldn't talk to her.	
Later, at home, Amanda was crying in her room. Her mom asked her what was wrong.	
Amanda said "Hannah and Jessica think I'm stupid and have been saying mean things to me." Amanda's mom asked her if she heard Hannah and Jessica say those things.	
Amanda realized she didn't. Amanda's mom suggested inviting the two of them over and asking them if they said those things, and why, if they did. She said that maybe some of the other girls were jealous about what good friends the three of them are and wanted to ruin it... She also said that a good friend would try to talk things out and not just believe someone else.	
Amanda called Hannah and Jessica. They met in the fort in her back yard. Jessica looked like she had been crying too. Amanda asked them why they had said mean things about her to Madison and they swore they never said anything like that. Amanda felt so bad that she told one of Jessica's secrets.	
They all cried and felt much better. The next day at school, Amanda told the other girls that she made up the secret about Jessica to see if Madison would spread it and that it wasn't really true. The three were back to being best friends and promised that in the future they would always talk things over instead of jumping to conclusions.	

Feelings Story #3

What happened...	How the person felt...
Robert and Adam were in the same class in school. They were both a little different from the other kids.	
Robert would get frustrated really easily and would lose his temper. Sometimes he even hit other kids and once he hit his teacher.	
Adam knew everything about coins and airplanes, but didn't always know what to say to the other kids or how to play with them. He would mostly play on his own or watch the other kids, except during gym class when he would try his hardest to win at everything.	
One day, Robert was sitting with Adam at lunch. Robert asked Adam what he did that weekend. Adam told Robert that he went to a birthday party on Saturday and his grandparent's house on Sunday. But then he didn't say anything else.	
So, Robert said, "Adam, now you are supposed to ask me what I did this weekend." Adam said, "Oh! What did you do this weekend?" and Robert told him. They kept talking about a lot of things and had fun together.	
Then, Robert had a few bad days at school. One day, he pushed a girl because she was in his way and hit a boy because he called Robert a name. Right after that, Adam broke his arm accidentally and came to school in a waterproof cast, which looked really interesting.	
Robert asked Adam if he could touch the cast, and Adam said, "Not today. I'm afraid you'll be too rough. But maybe you could try tomorrow if you don't hit anyone."	
For the first time, Robert realized that the other kids were watching him and felt scared even when he hit someone else. He tried very hard to use his words for the rest of the day and not hit anyone.	
Later, at karate, Robert was able to tell his teacher that he used self-control all day. She looked at him with a really big smile on her face.	
The next day, Adam came up to him and asked Robert if he wanted to touch his cast. Robert said, "Are you sure?" and Adam said, "Yes." So Robert touched the caste. It was bumpy and cool.	

My Own Story

In this space, you can write a story about something that happened to you. Maybe something upsetting happened, or a friend got mad at you and you didn't understand why. By breaking your story down into small sections, you might be able to better understand your feelings and the feelings of the other people involved. You might even think of a different way to handle the situation next time.

What happened...	How the person felt...

COMPLETION CERTIFICATE

has completed the feelings detective section of the workbook

_____
Signature

_____
Date

Feelings Scramble

Unscramble the feelings words, and then give an example of when you felt that way.

Scrambled Word	Unscrambled word	I felt that way when...
gyanr	_____	_____
ads	_____	_____
udopr	_____	_____
malc	_____	_____
ypaph	_____	_____
lynole	_____	_____
dipdsaointep	_____	_____
rurtsadfte	_____	_____
gear	_____	_____
sreemro	_____	_____
hasem	_____	_____
hys	_____	_____
lisyl	_____	_____
detir	_____	_____
predeseds	_____	_____
supet	_____	_____
xanious	_____	_____
rthu	_____	_____
pimtienta	_____	_____
oyj	_____	_____
olve	_____	_____

Feelings Ad Libs

Have you ever played the really fun game Mad Libs™? It's a fun game where short stories are missing key words. One person reads the story to herself (not out loud) while one or more other people supply words to finish the story without knowing anything about the story. All you need is a pencil, some knowledge of English grammar, and a great sense of humor. By the way, an "ad lib" is when people in show business just say what they want to say instead of sticking to the script. Here, you're just coming up with words off the top of your head and sticking them into stories.

If you don't know or have forgotten the meaning of adjectives, adverbs, nouns, and other parts of speech, then check the guide below for some hints.

Adjective: a describing word such as yellow, short, tall, grumpy, thick, hard, or messy. Most feelings words are adjectives, but some are verbs or adverbs.

Adverb: a word used to change another word, usually a verb, to show degree, place, manner, or time and usually ends with "ly". For example, usually, powerfully, thoughtfully, and lazily.

Exclamation: a word that is usually followed by an exclamation point! Examples include Wow! Ouch! Woah! and Yes!!

Location: a place. Could be a country or city, but also a room or anywhere you can be "in". Examples include Rhode Island, the bathroom, the car, the freeway, or in school.

Noun: a person, place, or thing. Chair, computer, girl, arm, boat, dog, and eye are nouns.

Plural: more than one. When asked for a plural noun, make it plural. For instance, finger becomes fingers.

Silly Word: usually a word that you make up, like scuzzball or floopy.

Verb: an action word. Run, jump, play, scream, and breath are all verbs.

Sometimes, we'll ask for a more specific word such as *number, name of a body part,* or *favorite book.*

Roller Coaster Ad Lib

One spring, Robert's family took a vacation to Disney World™. He was so _____!
(feelings word)

He'd never been to Disney World before and he'd never been on a _____.
(noun)

The flight took _____ hours but it felt like ten because he wanted to get there so badly.
(number)

The next morning they left for the Disney World park. Robert was _____and
(verb)

_____ and talking really fast. They rode the _____ into the park and slid their passes
(verb)   (noun)

through the _____. "Oh my _____! Look! It's the real Disney _____!"
(noun)   (exclamation)   (noun)

Robert exclaimed. His sister squealed in delight. They saw Cinderella and got in line to get her

_____. Robert and his sister got her autograph and got their _____taken
(noun)   (noun)

with her. It was a _____ come true for his _____.
(noun)   (noun)

Next, they got in line for Space Mountain™. The line was a little _____ this
(adjective)

time, so they played "_____" while they waited. Robert got a little _____,
(game)   (feelings word)

but got over it _____ because it was their turn to go on the roller coaster. And, wow, was it
(adverb)

_____. Dark and _____ and up and _____ and side to side!
(adjective)   (adjective)   (adjective)

_____! When they got out, Robert yelled "Let's go again and again and again!"
(exclamation)

His sister was _____, though, because she thought it was _____ and didn't want to
              (verb)   (adjective)

go on it again. Robert _____ his feet and called her a _____. Roberts's parents
                              (verb)   (noun)

were very disappointed in him and told him he should be more understanding. Robert apologized to his

sister and felt _____ – he was so excited he didn't stop to _____. Then, they
                    (adjective)   (verb)

worked out a compromise – Robert went on Space Mountain again with his mom, while his dad took

Robert's sister to get Snow White's autograph.

My Day at School Ad Lib

Like most other kids, I go to _____. My most favorite subject is _____
                                               (location)   (noun)

and my least favorite subject is _____, and that's if you don't count _____.
                                      (noun)   (noun)

Some days I'm very _____ in the morning, and other days I can't wait to get there to see
                              (adjective)

my friends.

My teacher is really _____ most of the time, although she does get a little _____
                             (adjective)   (feelings word)

when I don't raise my _____. She helps me remember by putting a _____ of a
                            (noun)   (noun)

raised hand on my _____. My teacher has us _____ in groups of _____ kids. In
                        (noun)   (verb)   (number)

our group, Emily is the _____ at reading and sometimes _____ me, and I'm the best at
                           (adjective)   (verb)

_____ and sometimes help the other _____. Our teacher says that when we _____
(noun)   (plural noun)   (verb)

each other, she doesn't have to work so _____.
                                   (adjective)

I used to _____ doing my homework. Well, I still hate doing _____ – I'd
                 (feelings word)   (noun)

rather be _____. But, if everyone in our _____ hands in all of our homework, we all get
             (verb)   (noun)

a free homework _____ the next week. I felt really bad when we didn't get the _____
                         (noun)   (noun)

because I didn't do my _____. It feels _____ when everyone gets a free pass, so now
                            (noun)   (adjective)

I do my homework.

I love a good story, especially a _____ one. It makes me so mad that reading is so

(adjective)

_____ for me. I get extra help though, and I'm starting to catch up to the other _____.

(adjective)   (plural noun)

I'll be glad when I am caught up and it gets _____. There are a lot of _____ I'd like

(adjective)   (plural noun)

to be able to _____ to myself!

(verb)

The best thing about _____ is seeing my friends. I used to get in a lot of _____

(noun)   (plural noun)

with other kids, but I do a better job now. I try to remember that it's OK to lose a _____ or get

(noun)

an out, and that it's more important to have a _____ than to be right. If I get really

(noun)

_____, I take some deep breaths or just _____ away for a while.

(feelings word)   (verb)

School gets _____ for me every year, but I still like the summer the most!

(adjective)

Playing in the Neighborhood Ad Lib

I live in a _____ neighborhood. Our street is a _____ -shaped street that is
         (adjective)   (adjective)

very _____ and has at least _____ houses on it. There are a lot of kids on our street
      (adjective)   (number)

and they all like to _____ outside.
                 (verb)

Some of the _____ are really young, and although they are _____, they aren't
            (adjective)   (adjective)

fun to play with for very long. I like _____ with kids who like to have _____ the
                           (verb)   (noun)

most. We can ride our _____ or our scooters, or _____ we are in a Star Wars movie.
             (plural noun)   (verb)

My sisters don't like to play _____; they like to talk a lot. Sometimes, they spend more
                         (movie)

time _____ about the rules for a _____ than it takes to play the game. _____!!
    (verb)   (noun)   (exclamation)

Other times, I have no one else to play with, so I do _____ with them.
                                        (verb)

Some of the _____ in my neighborhood are _____ and some of them are
             (plural noun)   (adjective)

not. The kids who are nice just like to _____ and have fun. They play by the _____
                              (verb)   (plural noun)

most of the time and they take turns. They also don't call the other kids _____ or do mean
                                                  (plural noun)

things to them. Some other _____ in our _____ are not nice at all. One time, Alex
                   (plural noun)   (location)

jumped out of a _____ dressed as the Scream just to _____ me and see what I
            (noun)   (verb)

would do. Other times, they try to trick me into buying a broken _____ or tell me my
(noun)

_____ friend doesn't like me anymore. Nick even told me that he would _____ with
(adjective) (verb)

me if I gave him _____. My sisters _____ him they wouldn't let me play with him even
(noun) (verb)

if he paid me! I like it when they are on my _____ and stick up for me.
(noun)

My _____ tell me it's better to _____ by myself than play with _____
(plural noun) (verb) (plural noun)

who aren't nice. I'm glad that there are mostly _____ kids in our neighborhood.
(adjective)

My Family Ad Lib

Hi. My name is _____ and I live with my mom and _____, _____
(proper noun)   (noun)   (number)

sisters and _____ brothers. I wish I had a little _____, but mom and dad say "we have
(number)   (noun)

_____ kids". We live in a _____ on a street with lots of _____.
(adjective)   (noun)   (plural noun)

We have a pet _____ named _____ and two _____. We used to have more pets, but
(noun)   (proper noun)   (plural noun)

they _____. My mom works part time so she can be home when we get home from _____.
(verb)   (location)

She does _____ stuff. My dad works in an _____ too, but he's around most of the time.
(noun)   (location)

Sometimes, my sisters are my best _____, and other times I wish I was an _____
(plural noun)   (adjective)

child. They _____ with me and read to me and can be a lot of _____, but they also talk too
(verb)   (adjective)

much and _____ me around. And when we go out to _____, they always want to be the
(verb)   (meal)

ones to pick the _____. They like me some of the time, but other times they wish I would just
(location)

leave them alone. They are _____ than me and they stick up for me if other _____ are
(adjective)   (noun)

mean to me. I really _____ my sisters.
(feelings word)

I have _____ grandmas and _____ grandpas. My grandma lives in
(number)   (number)

_____, so we only see her a couple of times a year. She is a lot of _____. I also have a
(location)   (adjective)

52

lot of aunts and uncles and a bunch of cousins. Most of them live _____, but some others in

(location)

Oklahoma, _____, and Oregon. I like it when we get together with our cousins, especially

(location)

when we go _____ or _____ at the beach together.

(verb)   (verb)

My favorite times with my family are when we go to the _____ or go on _____.

(location)   (noun)

Last spring, we went _____ – it was really fun. I also like it when we go out for _____.

(location)   (noun)

My least favorite times are when I _____ with my sisters or my cousin is _____ to me.

(verb)   (adjective)

It isn't always easy to get along with your _____, but I love them and they _____

(noun)   (feelings word)

me!

Feelings Face Match

Draw a line matching the feeling with the face.

Scared

Angry

Frustrated

Sad

Happy

Surprised

Calm

Worried

Feelings Word Search

J	E	B	U	L	Q	G	M	D	I	S	A	P	P	O	I	N	T	E	D
M	K	U	E	D	B	Q	X	M	Y	K	P	Q	G	G	M	Z	A	G	N
R	G	H	U	F	R	U	S	T	R	A	T	E	D	Y	O	P	X	V	R
B	G	P	A	I	L	O	I	M	P	A	T	I	E	N	T	R	E	C	V
F	T	M	J	P	P	Y	I	U	D	V	B	M	N	R	Q	W	C	S	I
O	J	K	S	G	P	R	O	U	D	B	A	D	Z	E	T	M	P	Y	U
B	V	E	K	L	M	Y	C	X	I	U	E	A	X	B	C	C	Y	B	H
H	E	D	A	R	S	T	R	E	S	S	E	D	O	U	T	K	M	L	A
C	W	D	E	R	O	B	R	F	U	S	S	Y	M	N	N	P	V	X	T
O	A	S	R	G	C	V	U	F	M	P	H	L	U	A	D	T	B	G	E
N	W	B	Y	U	M	M	N	Z	Q	A	R	T	R	S	A	E	D	U	Y
F	B	Z	M	R	L	O	Q	P	D	A	E	C	R	O	Y	H	W	U	M
I	W	O	P	N	C	S	E	B	A	S	Y	M	N	G	M	U	R	T	Y
D	A	Q	A	J	E	H	P	Y	S	F	M	X	C	A	E	R	E	E	R
E	W	A	N	A	C	R	T	R	R	E	C	V	B	U	Y	T	Q	C	R
N	B	N	I	D	S	E	I	N	C	O	N	T	R	O	L	R	Y	S	O
T	B	O	C	E	Y	Y	M	Y	A	I	E	A	E	I	O	U	U	Y	S
P	S	K	T	S	B	D	E	T	I	C	X	E	K	D	B	C	N	B	A
W	U	A	L	S	M	Y	E	B	U	L	Q	G	A	E	P	S	E	Z	V
U	R	A	R	A	T	T	E	D	R	A	G	E	A	R	A	Y	R	A	G
Y	P	V	O	R	A	G	I	Y	T	R	T	R	V	A	S	B	V	A	E
C	R	B	P	R	M	M	S	Y	M	N	H	J	B	C	H	K	O	L	T
S	I	U	S	A	S	L	S	S	E	W	P	Y	U	S	R	B	U	M	I
Y	S	A	E	B	H	A	H	A	N	N	O	Y	E	D	E	I	S	O	R
B	E	R	T	M	R	C	R	M	E	B	U	L	Q	G	Y	G	V	C	E
A	D	B	H	E	E	P	E	E	K	X	R	L	F	F	E	K	Y	I	D
M	A	D	G	G	Y	D	E	P	R	E	S	S	E	D	D	E	S	S	E
L	S	Y	M	N	E	N	R	S	T	A	A	I	V	E	B	U	L	Q	G
N	T	R	E	A	B	R	E	C	V	G	R	E	L	I	E	V	E	D	R
I	N	T	E	N	S	E	I	L	O	V	E	H	J	M	X	O	M	O	M

annoyed	bored	calm	confident
confused	cranky	depressed	disappointed
embarrassed	excited	frustrated	happy
hate	hurt	impatient	in control
intense	nervous	panic	proud
rage	relieved	sad	scared
sorry	surprised	stressed out	tired

Feelings Crossword Puzzle

Down

1. When something happens that you didn't expect
2. Peaceful
3. Even happier than happy
4. Feel let down
5. Full of joy
6. Violent anger
7. More than sad
8. Bothered or irritated
9. Unhappy, crying

Across

1. Dull, not interested
2. Angry about things not going right or your way
3. Intense excitement
4. Anxious about something that might happen
5. Intense affection
6. Feeling happy about something good you have done
7. A sudden overwhelming fear
8. Mad at someone or about something
9. Startled or frightened
10. Knowing that you can do something

Word List

Angry	Annoyed	Bored	Calm	Confident
Depressed	Disappointed	Euphoric	Frustrated	Happy
Love	Manic	Panic	Proud	Rage
Sad	Scared	Surprised	Worried	

Hint: Check the Glossary on page 89 for definitions.

COMPLETION CERTIFICATE

has completed the feelings fun pages section of the workbook

Signature

Date

Dealing with Feelings

Everyone needs help with their feelings sometimes. In this section, you will learn ways to control your feelings instead of them controlling you! If you want to get good at these, practice. Every time you practice, color in the star next to that suggestion. Try to focus on one or two strategies at a time so you can get really good at them.

Deep Breathing

☆ ☆ ☆ ☆ ☆ ☆ ☆ ☆ ☆ ☆

Why: It's amazing how a little oxygen can help you think clearly and relax.

How: Make sure your shoulders are low and relaxed (not hunched up to your ears), and breath in slowly and so full that your belly pops out. Don't puff out your chest—get the air all the way down to your belly. Take at least 5 deep, slow breaths, maybe even 10. If you can't slow down enough or making your breathing even, count while you breath in and while you breath out (in, 1-2-3, out, 1-2-3).

When: Use deep breathing as a relaxation exercise or any time you are frustrated, angry, panicked, confused, crying, or about to blow your top.

TO GET STARTED: Practice with a friend or your mom or dad right now, and start coloring in those stars! Then take some notes...

What works for me:_____

_____

_____

_____

_____

_____

_____

_____

Ask for Help

☆ ☆ ☆ ☆ ☆ ☆ ☆ ☆ ☆ ☆

Why: Because there are a lot of people who love you, and you are not alone. And, it makes people feel good to help other people.

How: "Can you please help me? I'm having a hard time with (*fill in the blank*)." Ask for hugs, a kind word, help tying your shoes, help with a frustrating problem, etc. Try to remember to use a nice voice.

When: Whenever you need it.

TO GET STARTED:

1. Think about something that is hard for you, like waiting in line or losing a game.

   _____

2. List the people you can ask for help from.

   _____

   _____

3. Come up with at least two different ways of asking for help.

   _____

   _____

   _____

4. Practice saying it out loud with the people you're going to ask for help from.

What works for me:_____

_____

_____

_____

Label Your Feelings

Why: If you really understand how you feel, it's easier to deal with the feelings. It's also easier to talk about them and problem solve, and it's easier for other people to know how you are feeling and help you out.

How: Think about what happened, and try to remember how you felt – what your face looked like, how your body felt, and the thoughts you were thinking. If that isn't enough, then go through the feelings pages and look at the descriptions to see if you can figure it out. If you still aren't sure, talk to an adult or a friend and they can help you figure it out.

When: Whenever you have strong feelings or are getting upset. It's also good to practice this when you watch TV, a movie, or read a book. This is a great way to practice figuring out how other people feel and how you feel because you are calm and not personally involved in the situation.

TO GET STARTED:

1. Think about a time recently when you were upset.

   _____

2. Try to remember what happened.

   _____

   _____

3. Try to figure out when you started feeling upset and what you were feeling.

   _____

4. Try to write down the feeling you had and why you had it.

   _____

   _____

You can also practice this when you watch TV by focusing on a specific character.

What works for me:_____

_____

Laugh

☆ ☆ ☆ ☆ ☆ ☆ ☆ ☆ ☆ ☆

Why: It takes fewer muscles than frowning, it feels good, and helps you relax.

How: Joke books, keep a diary of funny stories, or watch a funny T.V. show or movie.

When: As often as possible, especially when you are feeling sad or angry.

TO GET STARTED: Write down your two favorite jokes or funny stories right here! I'll even give you one to get you started.

How do you make a tissue dance? Put a little boogie in it!!

_____

_____

_____

_____

_____

_____

_____

_____

Take Good Care of Yourself

☆ ☆ ☆ ☆ ☆ ☆ ☆ ☆ ☆ ☆

Why: People with healthy lifestyles handle stress more successfully.

How: Eat three well-balanced, nutritious meals a day, take any medicine regularly, go to bed on time and wake up on time, get daily exercise, get outside for fresh air and sunshine, and drink enough fluids. Stay away from things that are unhealthy, such as too much junk food, violent TV or video games, or staying up too late too many days in a row.

When: Every day!

TO GET STARTED: Decide on at least one change to your lifestyle to make it healthier, such as eating breakfast every day, even when you aren't hungry.

How I'm going to take better care of me:_____

_____

_____

_____

_____

_____

_____

_____

_____

Relaxation Exercises

☆ ☆ ☆ ☆ ☆ ☆ ☆ ☆ ☆ ☆

Why: They are calming and help with anxiety and anger. Relaxation exercises reduce stress on a daily basis and are a good way to cope with problems. People who do relaxation exercises, such as meditation, have more of the chemicals that promote calmness and well-being in their bodies.

How: There are a lot of strategies, including:

➢ Tense and relax the muscles in your body, one at a time, starting at your feet and ending with your face. Then tense your whole body and relax your whole body.

➢ Listen to the sounds around you. When your mind wanders, bring it back to listening.

➢ Focus on your breathing, even saying "in" and "out" in your head to help concentrate.

➢ Listen to calming, soothing sounds, such as the ocean or rain.

➢ Imagine your problems are in a hot air balloon and blow them away.

➢ Take a warm bath or a long shower.

➢ Meditate.

➢ Repeat the following mantra: In, Out, Slow, Deep, Calm, Ease, Smile, Release, Pretty Moment, Wonderful Moment

When: Daily, before bed, or when you are angry or scared or nervous or upset

TO GET STARTED: Decide to try at least one relaxation exercise (or more!) for a week. If you like it, try it for a month, otherwise; try another one.

Which relaxation exercise I'm going to try first:_____

_____

What works for me:_____

_____

_____

Exercise

☆ ☆ ☆ ☆ ☆ ☆ ☆ ☆ ☆ ☆

Why: It increases breathing and oxygen to the brain, makes your body feel good, and helps your body make the brain chemicals that make you feel calmer and happier. Studies have shown that people who exercise on a regular basis have fewer problems with depression.

How: Any physical activity you enjoy that isn't dangerous and doesn't hurt someone—bike riding, playing soccer, running, swimming, walking the dog, gardening, hopscotch, riding a scooter, kickball, yoga, gymnastics, basketball, etc. Try a bunch until you find out which ones you like best and make you feel better.

When: Ideally, at least once a day for 30 minutes, or anytime you feel the need to move.

TO GET STARTED: Pick an exercise and go do it!

Which exercises I'm going to try:_____

_____

_____

_____

What works for me:_____

_____

_____

_____

_____

Think About It Differently

☆ ☆ ☆ ☆ ☆ ☆ ☆ ☆ ☆ ☆ ☆

Why: It's amazing how our thoughts affect how we feel about a situation. For instance, if another kid bumps into you and you think "no big deal" you don't get angry. But, if you think "that kid is always mean to me," you might get really upset.

How: Try to think of at least one other way to look at the situation. If your mom says you can't have candy, try thinking "it's not good for my teeth." If your friend can't come over, try thinking, "he must be really sad that he's throwing up."

When: You can practice any time. Use this strategy when you start feeling angry, embarrassed, hurt, or upset.

TO GET STARTED: Pick a situation that has happened in the past, and try to think of three different ways to think about it.

What I could think next time:_____

_____

_____

_____

_____

_____

_____

_____

Self Talk

☆ ☆ ☆ ☆ ☆ ☆ ☆ ☆ ☆ ☆

Why: Self talk is a way of talking yourself through a tough situation. It uses a different way of thinking about things, but is a little more than that. It's almost like being your own coach.

How: Let's say you are scared to meet new kids. You can tell yourself that every friend you now have was once a stranger, but that person turned out to like you. You can think about what you want to say and what you will do depending on what the other kid says. You can also think about the worst thing that could happen, and that even feeling hurt will be Ok because you already have friends and you know you are a nice person.

When: When you feel nervous or scared or like you don't have confidence in yourself.

TO GET STARTED: write down some things you can say to feel more confident and practice saying them (in your head or out loud)!

Positive things about me:_____

_____

_____

_____

_____

Times or situations when I might use self talk:_____

_____

_____

_____

Keep a Diary or Draw about Your Feelings

☆ ☆ ☆ ☆ ☆ ☆ ☆ ☆ ☆ ☆

Why: Scientists did research and found that people who wrote about their feelings every day were less depressed than those who did not.

How: Use a diary, a journal, a computer, or anything that makes you feel comfortable, but you must write about your deepest feelings, even if they are painful, for it to work. Some people draw pictures about their feelings instead of using words or in addition to words.

When: Every day or as often as you are comfortable doing it.

TO GET STARTED: Go find a notebook of any kind, or if you prefer to type, head to the computer and start writing. Don't forget to get real.

What works for me:_____

_____

_____

Say How You Feel

☆ ☆ ☆ ☆ ☆ ☆ ☆ ☆ ☆ ☆

Why: It helps you understand your feelings so you can deal with them without hurting yourself or someone else. A lot of the time, when we are angry, it's really a reaction to another emotion such as fear, embarrassment, or hurt. If you know how you feel, you don't have to get angry, and you can talk to others about it and let them know how you feel.

How: Whenever you feel an emotion, label it in your head. If you become upset, try to say out loud how you feel. Make sure you start by saying "I feel..." instead of starting with what the other person did. If you don't feel safe, then just say it in your head and think of ways to live with that feeling.

When: Especially when you are angry or hurt so you can understand what is really causing the emotion.

TO GET STARTED: The next time you feel a strong emotion, say it out loud, such as "I am angry!"

Think about times when you need to speak up:_____

_____

_____

Think about what you can say: "I feel _____ when _____ "

_____

_____

Write down what happened when you did it:_____

_____

_____

_____

Go to Your Happy Place

☆ ☆ ☆ ☆ ☆ ☆ ☆ ☆ ☆ ☆

Why: It helps you relax and feel good, even when you are upset. And it can keep you from doing or saying things you might regret later.

How: Think of somewhere or a time where you are happy or at least relaxed. Picture this place in your mind. You may even close your eyes (if it's safe) so you can really concentrate on your happy place.

When: Whenever you feel a really strong negative emotion, such as anger, frustration, hurt, or embarrassment. Try practicing it beforehand so you can do it even when you are upset.

TO GET STARTED: Think of your happy place and try to go there in your imagination!

My happy place is:_____

_____

_____

How I'm going to remember to try it:_____

_____

_____

What happened when I used my happy place:_____

_____

_____

_____

Create a Quiet Zone

☆ ☆ ☆ ☆ ☆ ☆ ☆ ☆ ☆ ☆

Why: It can help you relax when you are getting upset or can be a place to calm yourself down and get yourself "back together" when you've already gotten upset.

How: Usually, it's a place in your bedroom or even in your yard. It has to be somewhere that you can have a little bit of privacy. In a really cramped house, it could even be just putting on your headphones with relaxing music and closing your eyes. Keep whatever relaxation tools you need in your quiet zone – a relaxation tape, calm music, a good book, or a musical instrument.

When: Put it together today and use it whenever you need it.

TO GET STARTED:

Where my quiet zone will be:_____

_____

What I want to have in my quiet zone:_____

_____

_____

What I will say to anyone who comes into my quiet zone while I am trying to relax:_____

_____

_____

What happened when I used my quiet zone:_____

_____

_____

Draw, Paint, or Color

☆ ☆ ☆ ☆ ☆ ☆ ☆ ☆ ☆ ☆

Why: Some people can express themselves better through drawing than through words. Other people find the repetitive physical movements of painting to be relaxing, and other people find that they need to concentrate hard to paint and that that helps them relax.

How: Whatever is allowed in your house. You might also try the pages of geometric patterns or a mandala to color – the repetitive patterns can be very calming.

When: If it makes you happy, any time. Otherwise, try it when you are unhappy – it might make you feel better.

TO GET STARTED: Talk to your parents to find out what you can do, and then make a plan!

What kind of drawing or painting I'm going to do:_____

_____

_____

Where I'm going to do it:_____

_____

What rules I need to remember:_____

_____

_____

How I felt when I did it:_____

_____

_____

Apologize or Make Amends

☆ ☆ ☆ ☆ ☆ ☆ ☆ ☆ ☆ ☆

Why: It feels good and it makes the person you've hurt feel better. Everyone makes mistakes, but it's important to try to make up for it when you've hurt someone else, even if it wasn't on purpose.

How: If it's really hard for you, start with "You ok?" That way, the person knows you care, but you don't have to say the dreaded "sorry" word. Once you get better at it, practice saying "I'm sorry", "I didn't mean to hurt you?", "Can I do anything to make you feel better?"

When: Anytime you've done something that may have hurt someone else. You can apologize right away, or even later. Sometimes, it takes a while to cool off to be able to apologize properly. Or, you can do something to make up for what you did, like replace something you broke or just do something nice for that person.

TO GET STARTED: PRACTICE, PRACTICE, PRACTICE!

What I'm going to say:_____

_____

_____

Examples of times I should apologize:_____

_____

_____

What happened when I apologized:_____

_____

_____

_____

COMPLETION CERTIFICATE

has completed the dealing with feelings section of the workbook

_____
Signature

_____
Date

Charting

Have you ever heard of a mood chart? It's a way to keep track of your changing moods. Why is that important? Charting your mood changes helps you be more aware of your feelings and how they relate to your health. You may start noticing a pattern that can help you come up with a plan to even out your moods. Lastly the mood chart can help you appreciate all the times you feel good! I challenge you to chart your moods every day for a whole week. You will learn more than you think about yourself. So take the Charting Challenge today!!

On the following pages are a couple of different charts. The first is a two page chart that is designed for weekly use that includes pictures from "*My Bipolar Roller Coaster Feelings Book*" and from "*Brandon and the Bipolar Bear*". The front page is for charting and the back side has a key. Following that is one that is a daily chart, created by Tracy Anglada, including pictures from her book, "*Brandon and the Bipolar Bear*".

Finally, there is a list of web sites where you can find other charting tools.

Week Starting:

	Sunday	Monday	Tuesday	Wednesday	Thursday	Friday	Saturday
Morning							
Mood							
Energy Level							
Irritability							
Aggression							
Food?							
Took medication							
Afternoon							
Mood							
Energy Level							
Irritability							
Aggression							
Food?							
Took medication							
Evening							
Mood							
Energy Level							
Irritability							
Aggression							
Food?							
Took medication							
Hours of Exercise							
Hours TV/Comp/Video							
Time Woke Up							
Time to Sleep							
Comments							

*See 2nd page for moods and scales to use for energy level, irritability, and aggression. Medication is yes/no.

Mood examples:

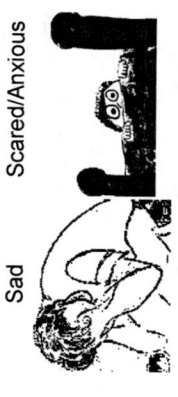     

Sad   Scared/Anxious   Good/OK   Happy   Hyper/Silly   Irritable   Angry

Energy level:
5. Can't stop moving, impossible to tire
4. A lot of energy, but can be appropriately channeled
3. Just right
2. A little low
1. Has no energy for anything other than watching TV

Irritability
5. Walking on eggshells, everything irritates and angers
4. Irritable most of the time, very negative
3. Irritable about 50% of the time
2. A little irritable, but easily joked out of.
1. No irritability

Aggression
5. Physically aggressive, hits, kicks, pinches, bites, etc.
4. Lots of threats, abusive language, throws things, does not harm people or animals
3. Threatens when upset, nothing physical at all
2. Pushy, demanding, loud, sarcastic
1. Not aggressive

79

My Mood Chart for _____

Name: _____

Today's date _____

In the morning I felt:
(circle all the ways you felt)

Sad/Depressed | Scared/Anxious | Sick/Yuck! | Good/ O.K. | Happy | Hyper/Silly | Angry/Irritable

In the afternoon I felt:

Sad/Depressed | Scared/Anxious | Sick/Yuck! | Good/ O.K. | Happy | Hyper/Silly | Angry/Irritable

In the evening I felt:

Sad/Depressed | Scared/Anxious | Sick/Yuck! | Good/ O.K. | Happy | Hyper/Silly | Angry/Irritable

Last night I fell asleep at _____ : _____   This morning I woke up at _____ : _____

Today I took all my medicine: (circle one)   on time   late   early   oops! forgot:

Last night I took my medicine: (circle one)   on time   late   early   oops! forgot:

New medicine I started or medicine I stopped: _____

Something I want to tell my doctor: _____

Other Charting Resources

There are many different ways of charting behavior and health. Following are some additional charts created by other resources, including one that is electronic. Or, make your own in Microsoft Word or Microsoft Excel!

Description	Web Address
Tracy Anglada's mood chart for boys (included)	http://www.bpchildren.com/pdf/MyMoodChart.pdf
Tracy Anglada's mood chart for girls	http://www.bpchildren.com/pdf/MyMoodChartforGirls2.pdf
Julie Ward's mood chart for boys	http://www.gcbf.org/resources/daily_chart_for_boys.pdf
Julie Ward's mood chart for girls	http://www.gcbf.org/resources/daily_chart_for_girls.pdf
Shelly's mood chart	http://www.bpkids.org/site/DocServer/shellysmoodchart.pdf?docID=200
Mass General Hospital	http://www.manicdepressive.org/images/moodchart.pdf
Psychiatry 24x7	http://www.psychiatry24x7.com/content/backgrounders/psychiatry24x7.com/blank_chart.pdf
Julie Ward's rainbow chart	http://www.gcbf.org/rainbow.pdf
Julie Ward's hourly chart (for rapidly cycling kids)	http://www.gcbf.org/hmm.pdf
Thermometer chart	http://www.gcbf.org/thermometer.pdf
Curlywhirley's mood charts	http://bpinfo.net/mood_chart.htm
Mood Diary from Zyprexa	http://zyprexa.com/pdf/MoodDiary.pdf
Zyprexa caregiver diary	http://zyprexa.com/pdf/CaregiverDiary.pdf
Electronic mood chart (Word version too)	http://www.psycheducation.org/FAQ/MoodCharts.htm

COMPLETION CERTIFICATE

has completed the charting section of the workbook

_____
Signature

_____
Date

Problem Solving

Sometimes, one of the best ways to prevent problems with feelings is to slow down and problem solve instead of going with your first reaction to a situation. On the following pages is a process and worksheet for solving problems. Flexibility and looking at the situation in different ways is very important in problem solving.

Problem Solving Process

1. Stop!

One of the most important things to do is to stop and think about the situation *before* you react. Try to understand what you are upset about and how important it really is to you. Also, just stopping often gives you the time to get past your first reaction and you may find you aren't so upset after all.

Activity: Color the top circle inside the traffic light red.

2. Think!

The first thing to think about is to understand the problem. Ask questions if you need to, so you can understand whether there even is a problem before you get upset. For example, your Mom says you can't have any candy. Maybe it's because it's almost dinner and she wants you to wait until after dinner, not that you can't have any candy for the rest of your life.

Activity: Color the middle circle inside the traffic light yellow.

Next, think about some solutions. Most of the time, there are many ways of working a problem out. If your friend doesn't want to share his new toy, you can take it from him, you can whine, you can stomp off and not play with him, you can ask for a turn, or you can decide it's OK and you'll play with something else.

Try to come up with at least three different solutions.

Next, throw out any solutions that are not safe. Don't ever pick a solution that hurts someone else. That is not working things out. In this example, you wouldn't take the toy away from your friend because he could get hurt.

Finally, decide which solution you want to try and try it! Try to pick the solution that will make the most people at least somewhat happy, rather than always putting your own needs first. It's often easier to work things out if you compromise.

3. Go!

Try out your solution!

Did it work? Are there any other times you think that solution would work? As you get better at problem solving, you'll get better at figuring out what solution is the best. But the only way to get better at it is to practice, practice, and practice!

Activity: Color the bottom circle inside the traffic light green.

Problem Solving Worksheet

1. Stop! *(color the top light red)* **How do I really feel about this?**

_____

_____

2. Think! *(color the middle light yellow)*

a. What is the problem?

_____

_____

b. What are some possible solutions?

_____

_____

_____

c. Are any unsafe? Throw those ones out!!

d. Pick one of the safe solutions. Write down the one you are going to use.

_____

_____

3. Go! *(color the bottom light green)*

_____

Did it work? _____ Why? Are there other situations you can use this solution for?

If no, which solution do you want to try next?

_____

_____

Sample Problem

Robert's family was planning to go out to dinner. Robert wanted to go to MacDonald's, but his sisters wanted to go to Kentucky Fried Chicken.

1. Stop! (color the top light red) **How do I really feel about this?**

Robert was frustrated that his sisters wouldn't go to MacDonald's and was disappointed he might not get to go there.

2. Think! (color the middle light yellow)

    a. What is the problem?

They want to eat in different places because they like different food.

    b. What are some possible solutions?

They could stay home and have soup.

They could go two different places.

They could go to the taco place where everyone can get something they like.

    c. Are any unsafe? Throw those ones out!!

    d. Pick one of the safe solutions. Write down the one you are going to use.

The taco place.

3. Go! (color the bottom light green)

Yahoo!

Did it work? Yes_____ Why? Because we compromised on a solution we could all live with.

Are there other situations you can use this solution for?

If no, which solution do you want to try next?

COMPLETION CERTIFICATE

has completed the problem solving section of the workbook

Signature

Date

Feelings Glossary

Active In motion, a lot of energy

Afraid Another word for scared

Angry Mad at someone or something

Annoyed To be bothered or irritated

Ashamed Feeling bad or embarrassed about something you've done

Astounded So surprised you don't even know what to say

Awesome Better than fantastic

Bitter Angry and disappointed

Bored Dull, uninterested, nothing to do

Brave Able to face danger without fear

Bubbly So happy, seem full of bubbles

Calm Not excited or agitated; peaceful

Cautious Watchful or careful

Confident Feeling certain, knowing that you can do something

Confused To be mixed up, in a jumble

Cranky Grouchy, irritable

Depressed Sad, bored, cranky, no energy, nothing feels or tastes good

Destructive To destroy, spoil, or ruin

Determined Feeling very strongly and firm about a decision

Disappointed To feel let down

Discouraged To have no confidence or courage

Disgusted A very strong dislike, yucky

Dramatic More emotion than is usual, like an actor on a stage

Embarrassed To feel bad about how you look or something you've done, sometimes causing feelings of shyness or shame

Empathy Understanding the thoughts or feelings of another

Encouraged Full of courage or hope

Enthusiastic Strong feeling for a subject or a cause, eagerness

Euphoric Even happier than happy, colors are brighter, and you love everything and everyone

Excited To be in action or motion, to have strong feelings

Exhausted Worn out

Fascinated Very interested in a topic or person

Flexible Able to change

Frustrated To feel angry about not being able to get your way

Glad Another word for happy

Great Very good, first rate

Guilt Feeling responsible for doing something wrong

Happy Feeling full of pleasure or joy

Hate To feel intense dislike or hostility

Hopeless To be without hope

Horrified To be very scared

Hurt To experience pain in your body or feelings

Hysteria Everything makes you laugh uncontrollably and you can't stop

Hysterical Your emotions are out of control – you may be laughing too hard or crying too hard or very upset over something small. Sometimes this word just means "very funny".

Indifferent Feeling like you don't really care one way or the other

Impatient Unwilling or unable to wait

In-control Able to control your actions

Indecisive Can't make a decision

Insecure Not confident or sure

Intense Extreme, very strong

Jealous Wanting what someone else has

Joy Great happiness, delight

Lonely Feeling all alone, missing someone

Love Intense affection

Mad Another word for angry

Manic Excessive and unreasonable emotional excitement and physical overactivity

Mixed Having more than one feeling, sometimes opposite feelings, at the same time

Motivated Feeling spurred to action

Nervous Worried, jumpy

OK Acceptable, just right

Optimistic Feeling very positive about things or people most of the time

Outraged Very angry about how someone has treated you or how something turned out. Feeling like it should have happened differently

Panic A sudden overpowering fear

Pleased Feeling happy about how something turned out

Proud Feeling very pleased or happy about something good you have done

Rage Violent anger

Regret Upset over doing the wrong thing

Relieved Freed from pain or trouble

Remorse Feeling bad about things you've done wrong in the past and wishing you could change it

Resentment To still feel angry about something that happened in the past

Responsible Having a duty or obligation, being dependable

Sad Unhappiness or regret

Scared To be startled or frightened

Shame Feeling bad because of guilt, a shortcoming, or having done something wrong

Shy Easily frightened, timid, or afraid to talk to people

Silly Foolish or goofy

Sorry Feeling bad about something you've done or for someone else

Startled Similar to surprised, usually sudden but not serious

Stupid Feeling like you aren't smart, lacking intelligence

Stressed out Total stress – can't take any more

Sure Feeling confident, without doubts

Surprised When something happens that you didn't expect

Thankful Showing or feeling thanks

Timid Fearful, lacking self-confidence

Tired Weary, sleepy, or bored

Trapped Feeling like there is no way out, like you have no other options

Unsure Not confident, full of doubt

Upset Feeling emotionally troubled, agitated, or disturbed

Worried Anxious about something that might happen

Fun Pages & Feelings Detective Answers

Feelings Stories

Feelings Story #1

What happened...	How the person felt...
One winter day, a lot of the kids in the neighborhood were playing in the snow. It had snowed a lot the night before and school was closed. Robert looked out the window and got his snow things on. He called to his sisters, "Get out of bed, there's a war going on out there!"	Robert was excited.
Robert headed out the door. Nick said, "Be on my team, it's boys against girls!" It was mostly the younger kids in the neighborhood and there were two snow forts with kids throwing snowballs at each other. No one was throwing the snowballs too hard and it was fun.	Robert was happy.
Robert's sisters came out and joined the girl's team. It was getting very competitive now and Robert got hit in the face once or twice. He was trying to stay cool, but it hurts getting hit in the face.	Robert was a little worried and a little happy.
Then, some of the older boys from the other end of the street came down to join in. Sometimes they were too rough for the younger kids.	Robert was more worried.
At first, it was fine, but then they started packing the snowballs really hard. When Robert got hit accidentally by a hard one, he started crying. The older boys started laughing and making fun of him.	Robert was hurt and then embarrassed.
Then, it got really out of hand. The older boys started throwing snowball after snowball at Robert and they thought it was funny. Roberts sister's said "That's more than enough!" While Nick put his sled in front of Robert to stop the snowballs from hitting him, Robert's sisters went and got their mom. The older boys scattered as soon as she opened the door.	Robert was starting to panic. Robert's sisters were angry. Nick was feeling protective. Robert's mom was angry. The older boys were nervous they would get in trouble.
The other kids all came around Robert and told him they felt bad about what happened and suggested that they make a snowman instead. They all worked together and made the biggest snowman ever.	Everyone felt bad for Robert. Robert felt good that the other kids still wanted to play with him. They all felt happy and proud about working together.

Feelings Story #2

What happened...	How the person felt...
Hannah, Jessica, and Amanda were best friends. They lived on the same street, went to the same school, and like a lot of the same things. They walked to school together every morning and walked home every afternoon.	All three girls were happy.
One day, Madison, another girl at school, told Amanda that Hannah and Jessica had been saying mean things about her and that they thought she was stupid. Amanda couldn't believe it—how could they do that to her?	Amanda was hurt and angry and disappointed.
So, the next day at school, Amanda told one of Jessica's secrets to Madison. Madison spread it to three other girls and one of them told Jessica that she knew. Jessica couldn't believe it—how could Amanda do that to her?	Amanda was angry. Jessica was hurt and embarrassed and angry and disappointed.
Hannah tried to talk to Amanda to find out what was going on, but Amanda wouldn't talk to her.	Hannah was hurt, Amanda was angry.
Later, at home, Amanda was crying in her room. Her mom asked her what was wrong.	Amanda was sad. Amanda's mom was concerned.
Amanda said "Hannah and Jessica think I'm stupid and have been saying mean things to me." Amanda's mom asked her if she heard Hannah and Jessica say those things.	Amanda was hurt.
Amanda realized she didn't. Amanda's mom suggested inviting the two of them over and asking them if they said those things, and why, if they did. Mom said that maybe some of the other girls were jealous about what good friends the three of them are and wanted to ruin it... Mom also said that a good friend would try to talk things out and not just believe someone else.	Amanda was surprised. Amanda was a little embarrassed.
Amanda called Hannah and Jessica. They met in the fort in her back yard. Jessica looked like she had been crying too. Amanda asked them why they had said mean things about her to Madison and they swore they never said anything like that. Amanda felt so bad that she told one of Jessica's secrets.	Amanda was nervous. All three girls were sad. Amanda was ashamed.
They all cried and felt much better. The next day at school, Amanda told the other girls that she made up the secret about Jessica to see if Madison would spread it and that it wasn't really true. The three were back to being best friends and promised in the future they would always talk things over instead of jumping to conclusions.	All three girls were happy. Madison was hurt and embarrassed.

Feelings Story #3

What happened…	How the person felt….
Robert and Adam were in the same class in school. They were both a little different from the other kids.	A little lonely.
Robert would get frustrated really easily and would lose his temper. Sometimes he even hit other kids and once he hit his teacher.	Robert was frustrated and angry.
Adam knew everything about coins and airplanes, but didn't always know what to say to the other kids or how to play with them. He would mostly play on his own or watch the other kids, except during gym class when he would try his hardest to win at everything.	Adam was confused and lonely.
One day, Robert was sitting with Adam at lunch. Robert asked Adam what he did that weekend. Adam told Robert that he went to a birthday party on Saturday and his grandparent's house on Sunday. But then he didn't say anything else.	Robert was curious. Adam felt good that Robert was interested in him.
So, Robert said, "Adam, now you are supposed to ask me what I did this weekend." Adam said, "Oh! What did you do this weekend?" and Robert told him. They kept talking about a lot of things and had fun together.	Adam was surprised. Both boys were happy.
Then, Robert had a few bad days at school. One day, he pushed a girl because she was in his way and hit a boy because he called Robert a name. Right after that, Adam broke his arm accidentally and came to school in a waterproof cast, which looked really interesting.	Robert was angry. Adam was hurt.
Robert asked Adam if he could touch the cast, and Adam said, "Not today. I'm afraid you'll be too rough. But maybe you could try tomorrow if you don't hit anyone."	Adam was afraid of Robert hurting him.
For the first time, Robert realized that the other kids were watching him and felt scared even when he hit someone else. He tried very hard to use his words for the rest of the day and not hit anyone.	Robert was surprised and embarrassed and sad.
Later, at karate, Robert was able to tell his teacher that he used self-control all day. She looked at him with a really big smile on her face.	Robert was very proud. Robert's teacher was proud and happy for Robert.
The next day, Adam came up to him and asked Robert if he wanted to touch his cast. Robert said, "Are you sure?" and Adam said, "Yes." So Robert touched the caste. It was bumpy and cool.	Robert was proud and happy. Adam felt happy too.

Word Search

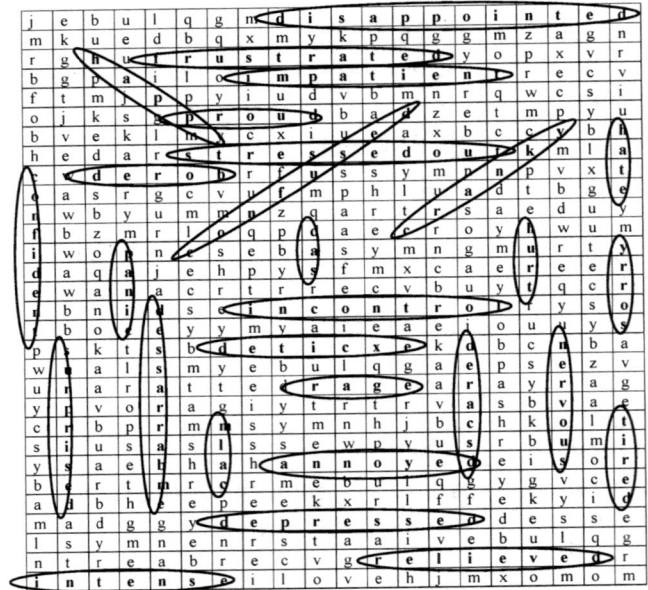

Crossword Puzzle

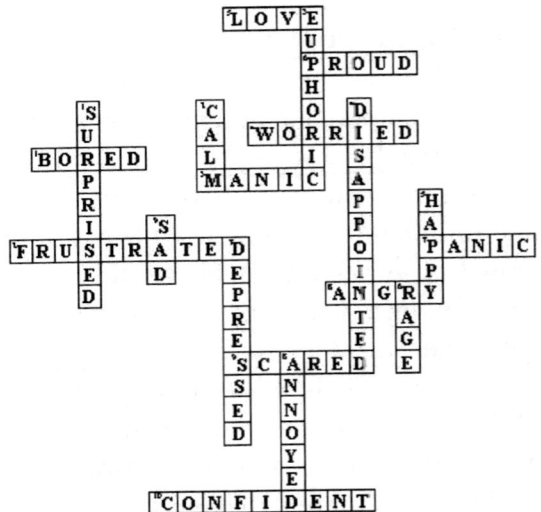

Face Match

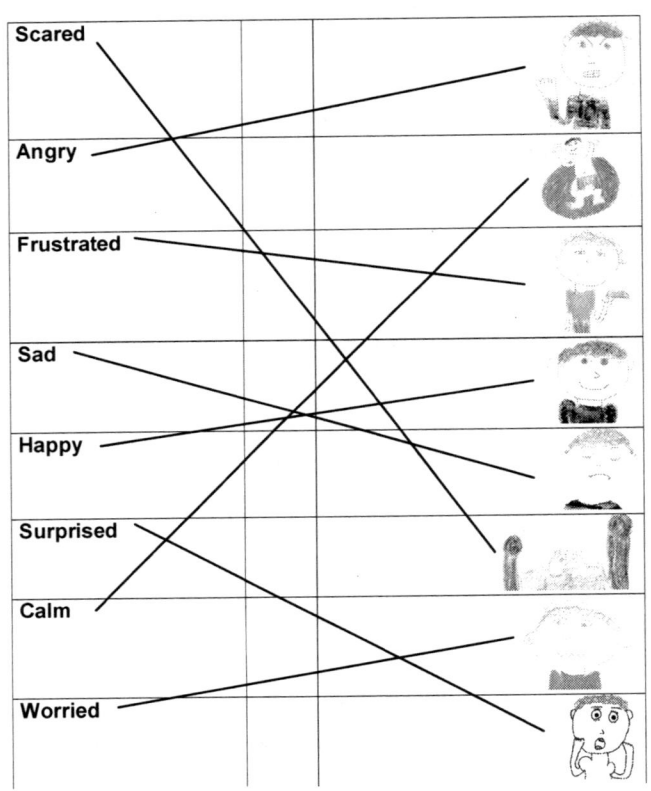

94

Feelings Scramble

Unscramble the feelings words, and then give an example of when you felt that way.

Scrambled Word	Unscrambled word
gyanr	angry
ads	sad
udopr	proud
malc	calm
ypaph	happy
lynole	lonely
dipdsaointep	disappointed
rurtsadfte	frustrated
gear	rage
sreemro	remorse
hasem	shame
hys	shy
lisyl	silly
detir	tired
predeseds	depressed
supet	upset
xanious	anxious
rthu	hurt
pimtienta	impatient
oyj	joy
olve	love

Feelings Ad Libs Answers

Roller Coaster Ad Lib (Completed story)

One spring, Robert's family took a vacation to Disney World™. He was so excited! He'd never been to Disney World before and he'd never been on a plane. The flight took three hours but it felt like ten because he wanted to get there so badly.

Robert was up at 5:00 am the next morning. Finally, they left for the Disney World park. Robert was skipping and jumping and talking really fast. They rode the tram into the park and slid their passes through the turnstile. "Oh my gosh! Look! It's the real Disney castle!" Robert exclaimed. His sister squealed in delight. They saw Cinderella and got in line to get her autograph. Thankfully, it was early and the line wasn't long. Robert and his sister got her autograph and got their picture taken with her. It was a dream come true for his sister.

Next, they got in line for Space Mountain™. The line was a little longer this time, so they played "famous person" while they waited. Robert couldn't concentrate, though, so he didn't win a single round. He got a little frustrated, but got over it quickly because it was their turn to go on the roller coaster. And, wow, was it fun. Dark and scary and up and down and side to side! Wheeeee! When they got out, Robert yelled "Let's go again and again and again!" His sister was crying, though, because she thought it was scary and didn't want to go on it again. Robert stomped his feet and called her a baby. Roberts's parents were very disappointed in him and told him he should be more understanding. Robert apologized to his sister and felt bad – he was so excited he didn't stop to think. Then, they worked out a compromise – Robert went on Space Mountain again with his mom, while his dad took Robert's sister to get Snow White's autograph.

My Day at School Ad Lib (Completed Story)

Like most other kids, I go to school. My most favorite subject is gym and my least favorite subject is reading, and that's if you don't count recess. Some days I'm very sleepy in the morning, and other days I can't wait to get there to see my friends.

My teacher is really nice most of the time, although she does get a little frustrated when I don't raise my hand. She helps me remember by putting a picture of a raised hand on my desk. My teacher has us sit in groups of six kids. In our group, Emily is the best at reading and sometimes helps me, and I'm the best at math and sometimes help the other kids. Our teacher says that when we help each other, she doesn't have to work so hard.

I used to hate doing my homework. Well, I still hate doing homework – I'd rather be playing. But, if everyone in our group hands in all of our homework, we all get a free homework pass the next week. I felt really bad when we didn't get the pass because I didn't do my homework. It feels better when everyone gets a free pass, so now I do my homework.

I love a good story, especially a funny one. It makes me so mad that reading is so hard for me. I get extra help though, and I'm starting to catch up to the other kids. I'll be glad when I am caught up and it gets easier. There are a lot of stories I'd like to be able to read to myself!

The best thing about school is seeing my friends. I used to get in a lot of fights with other kids, but I do a better job now. I try to remember that it's OK to lose a game or get out, and that it's more important to have a friend than to be right. If I get really frustrated, I take some deep breaths or just walk away for a while.

School gets better for me every year, but I still like the summer the most!

Playing in the Neighborhood Ad Lib (Completed Story)

I live in a big neighborhood. Our street is a horseshoe-shaped street that is very long and has at least 50 houses on it. There are a lot of kids on our street and they all like to play outside.

Some of the kids are really young, and although they are cute, they aren't fun to play with for very long. I like playing with kids who like to have fun the most. We can ride our bikes or our scooters, or pretend we are in a Star Wars movie.

My sisters don't like to play Star Wars; they like to talk a lot. Sometimes, they spend more time talking about the rules for a game than it takes to play the game. Sheesh!! Other times, I have no one else to play with, so I do play with them.

Some of the kids in my neighborhood are nice and some of them are not. The kids who are nice just like to play and have fun. They play by the rules most of the time and they take turns. They also don't call the other kids names or do mean things to them. Some other kids in our neighborhood are not nice at all. One time, they jumped out of a tree dressed as the Scream just to scare me and see what I would do. Other times, they try to trick me into buying a broken toy or tell me my best friend doesn't like me anymore. Nick even told me that he would play with me if I gave him money. My sisters told him they wouldn't let me play with him even if he paid me! I like it when they are on my side and stick up for me.

My parents tell me it's better to play by myself than play with kids who aren't nice. I'm glad that there are mostly nice kids in our neighborhood.

My Family Ad Lib (Completed Story)

Hi. My name is Robert and I live with my mom and dad, two sisters and no brothers. I wish I had a little brother, but mom and dad say "we have enough kids". We live in a house on a street with lots of neighbors. We have a pet dog named Tedy and two goldfish. We used to have more pets, but they died. My mom works part time so she can be home when we get home from school. She does computer stuff. My dad works more, but he's around most of the time.

Sometimes, my sisters are my best friends, and other times I wish I was an only child. They play with me and read to me and can be a lot of fun, but they also talk too much and boss me around. And when we go out to dinner, they always want to be the ones to pick the restaurant. They like me some of the time, but other times they wish I would just leave them alone. They are older than me and they stick up for me if other people are mean to me. I really love my sisters.

I have one grandma and no grandpas. My grandma lives in Chicago, so we only see her a couple of times a year. She is a lot of fun. I also have a lot of aunts and uncles and a bunch of cousins. Most of them live nearby, but some others live in Oklahoma, Chicago, and Oregon. I like it when we get together with our cousins, especially when we go ice skating or swimming at the beach together.

My favorite times with my family are when we go to the beach or go on vacation. Last spring, we went horseback riding – it was really fun. I also like it when we go out for ice cream. My least favorite times are when I fight with my sisters or my cousin is mean to me. It isn't always easy to get along with your family, but I love them and they love me!

Resources

Books	Organizations	Web Sites
Raising A Moody Child, Mary A. Fristad, Ph.D., Jill S. Goldberg Arnold, Ph.D.	Child & Adolescent Bipolar Foundation 1187 Wilmette Ave. Wilmette, IL 60091 Phone: (847) 256-8525 www.bpkids.org	All Kinds of Minds www.allkindsofminds.org
Intense Minds Tracy Anglada		American Academy of Child and Adolescent Psychiatry www.aacap.org
The Bipolar Child, Demitri Papolos, M.D. & Janice Papolos	NAMI Colonial Place Three 2107 Wilson Blvd., Suite 300 Arlington, VA 22201-3042 Phone: (703) 524-7600 www.nami.org	BPChildren: www.bpchildren.com
Straight Talk About Psychiatric Medications for Kids, Timothy E. Wilens, M.D.		Brainstorm: Your Pediatric Bipolar Infosource www.bpinfo.net
I'm Not Sick, I Don't Need Help, Xavier Amador, Ph.D.	The Saving Grace Foundation 124 Whipple Ave Barrington, RI 02806 Phone: 401-247-1888 http://www.thesavinggrace.com	Center for Effective Collaboration and Practice http://cecp.air.org
The Childhood Bipolar Disorder Answer Book, Tracy Anglada and Sheryl Hakala M.D.		Dr. Robert Brooks, Ph.D., Resilience, Self-Esteem, Motivation, and Family http://www.drrobertbrooks.com/
Easing the Teasing®, Judy S. Freedman	Federation of Families for Children's Mental Health 1101 King Street, Suite 420 Alexandria, Virginia 22314 Phone: (703) 684-7710 www.ffcmh.org	Easing the Teasing® http://www.easingtheteasing.com/
Helping Your Anxious Child, Rapee, Spence, Cobham & Wignall		Learning Disabilities Online http://www.ldonline.org/
Raising a Thinking Child, Myrna B. Shure, Ph.D.	National Institute of Mental Health (NIMH) 6001 Executive Boulevard, Room 8184, MSC 9663 Bethesda, MD 20892-9663 http://www.nimh.nih.gov/	Juvenile Bipolar Research Foundation www.bpchildresearch.org
The Explosive Child, Ross Greene, Ph.D.		National Association of School Psychologists www.nasponline.org
Winter Blues, Norman E. Rosenthal, M.D.		Online Asperger Syndrome Information & Support http://www.udel.edu/bkirby/asperger/
His Bright Light, Danielle Steele	National Mental Health Association 2001 N. Beauregard Street, 12th Floor Alexandria, Virginia 22311 http://www.nmha.org/index.cfm	School Behavior.Com www.schoolbehavior.com
Spinning Inward: Using Guided Imagery with Children, Maureen Murdock		Schwab Learning www.schwablearning.org
YogaKids: Educating the Whole Child Through Yoga, Marsha Wenig	STARFISH Advocacy Assoc. 17629 Scottsdale Blvd Shaker Hts., Ohio 44120 www.starfishadvocacy.org	Starfish Advocacy Association www.starfishadvocacy.org
Punished by Rewards, Alfie Kohn		The Bipolar Child www.bipolarchild.com
Wright's Law Books		The Reclaiming Youth Network www.reclaiming.com
		Wrightslaw www.wrightslaw.com

Survey

I'd love to get your feedback on this book.

Name (optional):_____   Email address (optional):_____

Age: _____   Role: ☐ Kid   ☐ Parent   ☐ Counselor   ☐ Other _____

What I liked most about this workbook: _____

_____

_____

What I found most useful: _____

_____

_____

The most important thing I learned was: _____

_____

_____

The least useful part of this workbook was: _____

_____

_____

If I could change anything in this workbook, it would be (& how): _____

_____

_____

Other comments: _____

_____

_____

_____

Please mail this survey to: Bryna Hebert, The Saving Grace Foundation, 124 Whipple Ave, Barrington, RI 02806 or email the answers to bryna.hebert@yahoo.com.

Ordering Information

Additional copies of *My Roller Coaster Feelings Workbook* can be obtained through www.bpchildren.com or by contacting:

Additional Titles Available Include:

My Bipolar Roller Coaster Feelings Book by Bryna Hebert A story about strong feelings for children with bipolar disorder (age 4-12).	
Anger Mountain by Bryna Hebert A story about managing anger for children (age 4-12).	
Brandon and The Bipolar Bear by Tracy Anglada A Story for Children with Bipolar Disorder (age 4-11) In paper and/or on DVD	
Turbo Max by Tracy Anglada A Story for Siblings and Friends of Children with Bipolar Disorder (ages 8-12)	
The Student with Bipolar Disorder by Tracy Anglada An Educator's Guide	
Pediatric Bipolar Disorder by Tracy Anglada A 22 minute DVD presentation on pediatric bipolar disorder	
I'll Chart My Moods 31 Days by Tracy Anglada One month sticker/mood chart.	

Lightning Source UK Ltd.
Milton Keynes UK
UKOW02f0656220414

230358UK00006B/416/P